How much yucky stuff do you know?

Collect all these gross fact books by Mitchell Symons!

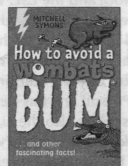 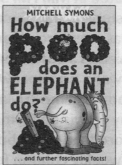

AVAILABLE NOW!

THAT'S SO GROSS! HUMAN BODY
A RED FOX BOOK 978 1 849 41190 5

Published in Great Britain by Red Fox,
an imprint of Random House Children's Books
A Random House Group Company

This edition published 2011

1 3 5 7 9 10 8 6 4 2

Mixed Sources
Product group from well-managed
forests and other controlled sources
www.fsc.org Cert no. TT-COC-002139
© 1996 Forest Stewardship Council
FSC

The Random House Group Limited supports the Forest Stewardship Council (FSC), the
leading international forest certification organization. All our titles that are printed on
Greenpeace-approved FSC-certified paper carry the FSC logo. Our paper procurement
policy can be found at www.rbooks.co.uk/environment.

Set in Optima

RANDOM HOUSE CHILDREN'S BOOKS
61–63 Uxbridge Road, London W5 5SA

www.kidsatrandomhouse.co.uk
www.rbooks.co.uk

Addresses for companies within The Random House Group Limited can be found at:
www.randomhouse.co.uk/offices.htm

THE RANDOM HOUSE GROUP Limited Reg. No. 954009
A CIP catalogue record for this book is available from the British Library.

Printed in the UK by CPI Bookmarque, Croydon, CR0 4TD

To all fans
of truly
GROSS trivia!

I TRODUCTIO

Welcome to a brand-new series of books which all have one thing in common: they're all intended to be ENGROSSING – with the emphasis on the third, fourth, fifth, sixth and seventh letters.

I've selected facts that are particularly gruesome in the hope that you will be disgusted and entertained in equal measure. Occasionally – very occasionally – I have used a fact from one of my other books (there's a list on page two but my editor and I know them fondly as 'Bum', 'Bogeys', 'Poo', 'Farts', Ear Wax', 'Puke' and 'Loos'). I've only done this where it fits in so perfectly that not to do it would be even worse!

There are three other books in this series. If you get them all, then you'll know as much as I do – or, indeed, *more* because as soon as I discover a new fascinating fact, I promptly forget at least two old ones! I think my brain's storage section has reached its full capacity.

As usual, I have a lot of thank yous. The most

important people are (in alphabetical order): Nigel Baines, Lauren Buckland, Penny Chorlton, Dominica Clements, Annie Eaton, Charlie Symons and Jack Symons.

In addition, I'd also like to thank the following people for their help, contributions and/ or support: Gilly Adams, Luigi Bonomi, Paul Donnelley, Jonathan Fingerhut, Jenny Garrison, Bryn Musson, Mari Roberts, Louise Symons and Rob Woolley.

As I always write at this point, if I've missed anyone out, then please know that – as with any mistakes in the book – it is, as ever, entirely down to my own stupidity.

Mitchell Symons

www.mitchellsymons.co.uk
www.grossbooks.co.uk

ENGROSSING BODILY FUNCTIONS

When people are trying to emphasize the importance of family over friends, they'll say: 'Blood is thicker than water.' But is it? Well, yes and no! Blood is thicker than fresh water, but is not thicker than sea water. In fact it's said that, in terms of chemical composition, the substance that human blood resembles most closely is sea water.

Fingernails grow four times faster than toenails.

Because of their elasticity, human lungs are a lot easier to blow up than a balloon.

If you've got a newborn baby brother or sister, you might have noticed flakes of . . . well, *something* on their scalp. This is cradle cap, an encrustation, that is caused by leftover chemicals from the mother's body. They cause oil glands in the baby's scalp to become active after birth.

As you get older you lose your taste buds. Your granny probably has only half as many as you do! You remind her of this when she's trying to tell you that something that you find too spicy isn't very spicy at all!

Snoring is no joke – especially for the sleeping partners of sufferers. Great snorers in history have included Abraham Lincoln, King George II and Benito Mussolini. 'Laugh and the world laughs with you; snore and you sleep alone,' declared the writer Anthony Burgess, while Mark Twain wondered why 'there ain't no way to find out why a snorer can't hear himself snore'.

Eventually, most men – and a lot of women – will snore regularly (and/or grind their teeth in their sleep, which is just as annoying for anyone unlucky enough to share their bed, room or even home!). Normal snores are as noisy as a person's ordinary speaking voice but some mega-snores can be almost as loud as a pneumatic drill.

Noise is one of the great blights of modern life. The trouble is that one person exercising their 'right' to (say) listen to loud music is interfering with another person's right to peace and quiet.

But noise is even more troublesome to people who do intricate work with their hands. Even small noises cause the pupils of the eyes to dilate. It is believed that this is why surgeons, watchmakers and others who perform delicate manual operations are so bothered by uninvited noise. The sound causes their pupils to change focus and blurs their vision, making it harder to do their job well.

Our stomachs contain hydrochloric acid to break down what we eat and drink and help some of our digestive enzymes to work. This acid is so strong that it could dissolve an iron nail.

Your stomach has to produce a new layer of mucus every two weeks to protect its walls so that it doesn't digest itself.

The human heart has enough pumping pressure to squirt blood nine metres.

The most common disease in the world is tooth decay.

When you sneeze, your heart stops momentarily.

Every year 8,000 people injure themselves while using a toothpick.

Human bones can withstand being squeezed twice as hard as granite can. Bones can also stand being stretched four times as much as concrete can.

The average human body contains enough iron to make an eight-centimetre nail, enough potassium to fire a toy cannon, enough carbon to make 900 pencils and enough phosphorus to make 2,200 match heads.

If 20-a-day smokers inhaled a week's worth of nicotine at once they would die instantly.

People who smoke have 10 times as many wrinkles as people who don't smoke.

Every year 100 people choke to death on ballpoint pens.

The brain itself can't feel pain. While the brain is the pain centre of your body and registers the pain of an injury, it doesn't have any pain receptors and so can't register its own pain. How ironic is that!

This explains how brain surgery is sometimes performed on patients who are fully conscious (necessarily so since the surgeon gains valuable information by the patient's responses).

The body's longest internal organ is the small intestine, with an average length of six metres. It has to be looped back and forth upon itself to fit inside you.

By confusing comparison, the *large* intestine is only a sixth of the length of the small intestine, but it is wider.

As important as they are, you don't need all your internal organs to survive. You could actually carry on living with the removal of your spleen, (almost all) your stomach, most of your intestines, one of your kidneys and one of your lungs. Mind you, you probably wouldn't feel all that good!

ENGROSSING BODILY MALFUNCTIONS

This is one of those facts that gets more gross each time you read it. According to researchers, when patients are brought into hospital 'dead on arrival', the people who work in accident and emergency departments are more likely to make resuscitation attempts on the good-looking patients than on the ugly ones. Isn't that awful? I'd be all right, of course, but I can't help worrying about all my (less good-looking) friends!

Asking for a second opinion (that is, an opinion from a different doctor) isn't a bad idea. In a survey, one out of every four second opinions failed to uphold the original doctor's opinion.

There is a disease called hypertrophy of the tongue that can make the tongue so large that it no longer fits into a person's mouth.

Epilepsy is a disorder that sometimes causes sufferers to have unprovoked (and therefore unpredictable) seizures. Sufferers in history include Julius Caesar, Alexander the Great, Vincent van Gogh, Napoleon, Leonardo da Vinci and Charles Dickens.

One epileptic described his condition this way: 'A seizure is like flushing a toilet in your brain.' Fortunately, these days, for many people epilepsy can be controlled by drugs. For those sufferers for whom drugs don't work, there's also the possibility of seizure-alert dogs, which can warn of an imminent attack by responding to subtle changes in human behaviour before someone has a seizure. What wonderful creatures those dogs must be!

We hear a lot about tooth decay but what exactly is it? Well, when you eat sweets, sugar-loving bacteria move in and break down the sugar on your teeth. These bacteria create acid, which eats away the enamel on your teeth. It also destroys some of the healthy bacteria that protect your teeth and starts the decaying process. That's why you must clean your teeth properly – otherwise you'll get cavities, which will need filling. If a tooth gets really rotten, a pus-filled hole, or abscess, can form underneath it. Sometimes germs from this abscess attack the gums and form a gum boil. If this bursts, it will fill the mouth with vile-tasting pus. Yeughh! I'm going straight to the bathroom to brush my teeth . . .

Do you know the difference between being 'chronically' ill and 'acutely' ill? A chronic illness is one that lasts a long time; an acute illness is a short, sharp one – or possibly a nasty intense part of a chronic illness.

There's a rare mental condition called multiple personality disorder. It does what it says on the packet: sufferers have different 'people' or personalities inhabiting their minds. Here's an extraordinary aspect to this disorder. If a sufferer has one personality who is diabetic and another who isn't, they can change between needing insulin regulation and not needing it, depending on which personality is active. The power of the mind, eh?

Doctors cut open dead bodies to check for causes of death – or just out of medical curiosity. These procedures are called post mortems or autopsies. When British doctors opened up soldiers killed in the First World War, they found no arteriosclerosis (the blocking of the blood vessels with cholesterol). American doctors carrying out autopsies on soldiers killed in the Vietnam War 50 years later found arteriosclerosis in almost all the bodies, even though many of the men were under 20 years old. The cause, they concluded, was increased consumption of junk food. It must be even worse today.

Warts – skin infections caused by viruses – are more common in children than they are in adults. They can affect any part of the body, but tend to invade warm, moist places, like small cuts or scratches on the fingers, hands and feet. They're usually painless unless they're on the soles of the feet (verrucas) or another part of the body that gets bumped. You can get warts from touching something someone with a wart has touched.

You'll be pleased to know that children get rid of warts quicker than adults. The best way to do it is to starve them of air so that they die. Home-grown remedies include covering them with plasters or (clear) nail varnish, but you can also buy very effective treatments from the chemist. There were lots of old-fashioned superstitious remedies to get rid of warts too. My favourite is rubbing them with a peeled apple and then feeding the apple to a pig!

Polydactyly is the condition where a person has more than five fingers on a hand or five toes on a foot. Where they have precisely six instead, the condition is also known as hexadactyly. Legend has it that Anne Boleyn, Henry VIII's second wife, suffered from this disorder on one hand, but an 1857 exhumation of her body disproved it. However, the actress Gemma Arterton was born with six fingers on each hand – as was the legendary West Indian cricketer, Sir Garfield Sobers. Both of them had those extra fingers removed.

Kidney stones are formed when dissolved salts in urine in the kidneys crystallize into a solid lump. I can tell you – from bitter experience – that the pain caused by these stones is absolutely excruciating. The largest known kidney stone apparently weighed 1.36 kilograms!

Leontiasis – or lion face – is a rare condition in which the facial and cranial bones in the skull overgrow. This can lead to total blindness due to compression of the optic nerve.

The letters 's', 'p' and 't' – all the consonants in the word 'spit' – produce the sounds most likely

to cause someone to spit when saying them and therefore pass on viruses, like colds and flu.

We need sleep as much as we need food – in fact more so! If you took two people and deprived one of food and the other of sleep, the one deprived of sleep would die sooner.

Not if he doesn't wipe that smirk off his face!

In an experiment, a computer program and real-life doctors were asked to diagnose people with various already identified problems. The computer program was right in 98 per cent of cases. By contrast, the doctors were right in just 78 per cent of cases.

The longest recorded bout of hiccups lasted for 65 years. That's not a 'bout', that's a lifetime!

Alexander Labret, a diver, was thrilled when he found a great shipwreck. He was going to be incredibly rich! Every day he went down 50 metres to salvage the treasures from the wreck – making more than 30 dives. As an experienced diver, Labret knew that he had to come up slowly from the wreck in order to avoid the bends, the name given to decompression sickness, a painful and dangerous condition in which bubbles of nitrogen appear in the blood and block circulation. However, on his very last dive, Labret was so excited that he came up more quickly than he should have done and suffered the bends so badly that he ended up paralysed for life. He had gained $350,000 of treasure but had lost control of his limbs.

The longest recorded sneezing fit lasted for 978 consecutive days. That's nearly three years! Bless you indeed!

As you know, we shiver when we're cold (it's an attempt by the body to warm us up), but if shivering bothers you, there is a (kind of) cure. Try adding up numbers in your head! No, honestly, medical researchers found that volunteers stopped shivering when they were given lists of numbers to add up.

Over 90 per cent of diseases are caused or complicated by stress.

Prior to the use of antibiotic drugs, such as penicillin, mouldy slices of bread were sometimes used to stop wounds from becoming infected. Antibiotic agents in the mould helped to combat infection.

Here are some irregular celebrities:

When Will Carling was captain of the England rugby union team, he couldn't cross his legs because they were too muscular.

Actress Geena Davis has an elbow that bends the wrong way.

The actress Whoopi Goldberg acquired her first name because she had a problem with flatulence.

Actress Darryl Hannah has a prosthetic fingertip – she lost the tip of her left index finger in an accident when she was three.

Actress Brenda Blethyn was born with an extra finger.

Actor Ashton Kutcher has two webbed toes on his left foot.

Actor Matthew McConaughey claims he hasn't worn deodorant in 20 years.

Here are some gross occupational hazards. Thankfully, most are from the past.

Aviator's Disease (altitude sickness)

Cheese Handler's Lung (caused by inhalation of cheese mould during the cheese aging process. Effectively, sufferers were overdosing on a form of penicillin)

Clergyman's Sore Throat (from all those sermons!)

Confectioner's Disease (damage done to the hands and nails of people who made sweets and so had their hands constantly immersed in hot sugar and syrups)

Farmer's Lung (caused by inhaling mouldy hay dust)

Housemaid's Knee (caused by working on their knees)

Mushroom Worker's Lung (caused by inhalation of mould spores from mushroom beds)

Painter's Colic (severe stomach aches caused by lead poisoning from lead in paint)

Peapicker's Disease (Weil's disease – caused by contact with rats)

Policeman's Disease (damage done to the soles of the feet from too much walking)

Potter's Bronchitis (caused by the inhalation of clay and dust)

Poultryman's Itch (skin disease from exposure to the parasites in chickens)

Railway Brain (mental problems caused by the strain of driving trains)

Washerwoman's Itch (hand problems caused by constant exposure to soaps and detergents)

ENGROSSING
FOODS

In other books, I've told you about some extraordinarily gross foods from around the world. Dishes like Sheep's Feet with Yoghurt (from Turkey) and Ox Palates in Browned Sauce (a French dish). Well, here are some more – and none of 'em are any less disgusting (or should that be 'dishgusting'?).

Stir-fried Dog (China)

Rabbit Excrement (Native Americans of Lake Superior used this as a flavouring in red wine)

Minced Giant Bullfrog Savoury Sandwich Spread (USA)

Deep-fried Horse (Switzerland)

Mixed Organ (spleen, pancreas, aorta, etc.) Beef Stew (Austria)

Roast Wallaby (Australia)

Calf's Head with Brain Fritters (19th-century USA)

Steamed Cat and Chicken (China)

Burgoo (squirrel, rabbit, pigeon, wild duck and/or chicken and vegetable stew) (Appalachia, USA)

Bandicoot Stewed in Milk (Australia, early 20th century)

Pork Intestines with Fish Cake and Liver (China)

Pea Soup with Pigs' Ears (Germany)

Tripe Soup (Czech Republic)

Pigs' Tails (France)

Smoked Dog (Philippines)

Dragon, Phoenix and Tiger Soup (snake, chicken and cat) (China)

Baked Opossum (USA)

Calf's-Foot Stew (Philippines)

Stewed Veal Shins (Italy)

Pot-roasted Cow's Udder (France)

Bears' Paws Dalmatian Style (Croatia and Dalmatia)

Dog Ham (China)

Pigs' Ears (Germany)

Baked Elephant Paws (Africa – 19th century)

Meanwhile, these meals can actually be bought in cans!

Smoked Rattlesnake

Buzzard Gizzards

Bamboo Worms

Southern Surprise Potted Possum Sauce

Bug Chilli Paste

Pure Texas Armadillo (sun dried and tenderized!)

King Oscar Fish Balls

Weaver Ants Eggs

Thai Green Curry with Crocodile

Brown Curry Mole Crickets

Golden Horse Powdered Horse Milk (not ponies)

Whole Baby Conch

Smoky BBQ Roasted Scorpions

Cajun-style Alligator

Spring River Villa Roasted Finless Eel

Armour Pork Brains in Milk Gravy

Roasted Crickets with Eggs

Preserved Black Scorpions

Many people – including people in the UK – consider brains (from calves or lambs) a delicacy. The brains have to be soaked in cold water, changing the water twice, after which the membranes are removed before cooking. Soaking makes them softer – otherwise they are too tough to be edible, though in some countries there's a tradition of eating them raw.

Eating brains isn't necessarily the, er, brainiest thing to do. Besides the high fat content of brains, there's also the risk of contracting fatal conditions – like variant CJD, the human version of mad cow disease.

During the Great Arkansas Pig-out, there's a contest called Running of the Fat Guys. Contestants weighing between 110 and 135 kilograms run through three checkpoints, where they have to guzzle pizzas, cola and bars of chocolate. I only have to put on a dozen kilograms or so and I'll be eligible to enter!

The Tomatina Festival in Bunol, Spain, sees the whole town throwing tomatoes at one another.

ENGROSSING SKIN

Let me tell you about scabs and why picking them is a particularly gross thing to do. Previous readers – and a big welcome back to both of you – will know this already and can safely wander on to another section while the newbies read on.

The skin has a wonderful way of healing itself – if you let it. Whenever you damage your skin, special blood-cell fragments, called platelets, help fix the damage. They rapidly stick together like glue at the cut, forming a clot. The clot forms a safe and protective 'plaster' made of human tissue over the wound, which stops more blood and other fluids leaking out. The clot uses other blood cells and thread-like stuff called fibrin to help hold the clot together.

Left alone, the clot gradually hardens and then dries out to form a scab, which is usually crusty and dark red or brown. The scab protects the wound by keeping germs out while the skin underneath gets busy repairing. As well as new skin cells, any damaged blood vessels are also being fixed. White blood cells, the ones that help fight other infections, zoom in to attack any germs that might have sneaked into the wound, especially from mud or dirt or contaminated water. These white blood cells also get rid of any dead blood and skin cells that may still be hanging around the cut.

Eventually, if you leave it alone to get on with it, usually after at least a week (but maybe longer if it is bigger and thicker), the scab falls off and underneath – hey presto! – there is brand-new skin. However, if you pick the scab (and, yes, I know it's unbelievably tempting), you can undo the repair and rip your skin again, which means it'll probably take longer to heal and, worse than that, if your fingers are dirty, or you expose the wound to further bugs, it may get infected. If you keep picking at it (now *don't*) you may even get a scar. So, tempting though it is to pick away (*stop it!*), it really is best to leave well alone and allow your body to heal itself and the scab to come away when it's ready.

An adult's skin could cover an area as large as two square metres if it were taken off the body. However, I wouldn't advise taking *any* skin off an adult as they really wouldn't like it.

About 10 billion tiny flakes of skin come off your body every day. These flakes don't weigh very much but, over a lifetime, *each one of us* sheds around 20 kilograms of dead skin.

If you're wondering where all these skin flakes go to (and if you're not wondering then maybe you should start), the answer's very simple. They become ordinary household dust that you see all around you. So the next time you look at the windowsill and see some dust, bear in mind that it's almost certainly part of you or, at the very least, related to you!

There's a good reason why we shed and regrow skin (usually on a monthly basis). It's essential that our skin is strong so that it can protect our internal organs. Regrowth ensures that it stays in tip-top condition. That helps to explain why elderly people's skin becomes wrinkled. They shed skin but it doesn't regrow so effectively. The subcutaneous (that means 'under the skin') layer also thins, making their skin less elastic and inclined to wrinkle.

You want to avoid sunburn, you really do. Even a little bit can seriously damage your blood vessels – to the extent that it can take more than a year for those blood vessels to return to normal. So when your mum is pestering you to wear a sunhat or telling you to stand still while she applies sunscreen, you should listen to her because sunburn is REALLY gross!

Scarification, the ritual application of scars on the faces of tribal members, is practised by many groups in Chad, Africa. Lines and other symbols are made on the faces of young men to mark them permanently as members of a particular tribe.

Why do we get spots, and what exactly is acne?

I'm sorry to have to be the one to tell you this, but you know those teenagers with their awful spots? Well, one day you might very well be one of them! There's no telling who's going to be the unlucky one with the pizza face. It used to be thought that it was all down to what foods people ate and how careful they were about keeping their faces clean, but although these

factors have a very small effect on your skin, it's really down to luck. Your skin is covered with tiny hair follicles, each with a gland that produces an oily substance called sebum. An excess of sebum causes spots. But what causes an excess of this sebum? The answer, I'm sorry to tell you, is hormones (the things that help humans to go from being children to adulthood).

Teenagers – especially boys – suddenly find their skin over-reacting to hormones, especially the male hormone, testosterone. This explains why more teenage boys than girls suffer from spots. Basically, what happens is that the hormones cause the glands to produce more and more oil, which mixes with dead skin cells and blocks the follicles. An infection then builds up behind this blockage and that's what causes spots.

Spots – blackheads, whiteheads or pimples or zits – look horrible, especially when they're 'angry', – that is, red and inflamed, which is, of course, more likely if you pick at them.

But who can resist picking or squeezing spots?

I can't, – or rather, *couldn't* in the days when I used to get them – and, if I'm honest (which I always am – honestly!), it took a supreme effort of will not to squeeze my sons' spots when they were teenagers. A great big spot full of pus is just asking to be popped or else it'll explode!

However, tempting though it might be, it's not always a good idea to pop spots as the very act of doing so can cause infection – especially if your fingers aren't clean – with the risk of leaving a permanent scar.

If you do pick them, make sure you don't press too hard, which can lead to redness and scarring. The best way is to use a swab of cotton wool dipped into recently boiled water and, when it's not too hot, press it against the spot. This should bring it to the boil, quite literally, and help it to explode. Do this very carefully as you don't want to burn your face as well. Someone with nice clean long nails is probably the best person to remove blackheads, though tweezers can also do the trick.

But the only spots really worth popping are those that have a yellow pus head, which you can squeeze out. You need to make sure you remove any yellow from the spot: if you leave any in there then it might come back.

So what exactly is pus? It sounds revolting but it's actually really important because it's your body's way of dealing with bad bacteria. It's a combination of white blood cells, dead bacteria and bits of old skin from the wound, which your body isolates in the spot to keep it away from your body. This is what you get when you squeeze a spot!

Acne is more persistent. That's why it has a special name! If breakouts of spots are consistent and almost impossible to get rid of, then they get to be called acne – and if you're unlucky enough to be prone to acne (it's all to do with your genes), you're just going to have to put up with it. Although, these days, there are powerful medicines available from the doctor to lessen the effects of acne.

Bear in mind, though, that the curse of acne needn't ruin your life. All the people listed below had acne in their youth, and what do they have in common? That's right, they all went on to become very successful!

Keira Knightley
Victoria Beckham
Jack Nicholson
Mike Myers
Rob Brydon

ENGROSSING SPIT

The mouth produces a litre of saliva a day. In the course of a lifetime, you'll produce enough spit to fill a swimming pool.

In 1965 a Scottish man coughed up just over 1.5 litres of phlegm in a single session.

In Tanzania, Africa, the Masai people regard spitting as a show of good will. Newborn babies are spat upon for good luck. Deals are often closed with a spit-soaked handshake.

Whenever you talk, you spray about 300 droplets of spit.

ENGROSSING PHOBIAS

A phobia is an irrational, intense, persistent fear of certain situations, activities, things or people. The key words are 'intense' (it can take over a person's life) and 'irrational' (it might make sense to fear snakes if you're in the jungle – but in the middle of a city?).

Here is a list of just *some* of the phobias identified by psychologists, and remember, if many of them seem strange – or even funny – to us, they've been tormenting someone, somewhere, enough for them to seek help.

Bear in mind also that many of these objects of phobia have their fans too. So someone who fears cats is an ailurophobe but someone who *loves* cats is an ailurophile ('phile' comes from the Greek for 'loving').

Ablutophobia – fear of washing or bathing

Achluophobia – fear of darkness

Agoraphobia – fear of open spaces or of being in crowded, public places, such as markets. This can lead – like so many phobias – to the sufferer being unable to leave their home

Alektorophobia – fear of chickens

Arachnophobia – fear of spiders

Barophobia – fear of gravity

Bibliophobia – fear of books

Brontophobia – fear of thunder and lightning

Bufonophobia – fear of toads

Catoptrophobia – fear of mirrors

Chorophobia – fear of dancing

Claustrophobia – fear of confined spaces

Clinophobia – fear of going to bed

Coulrophobia – fear of clowns

Dendrophobia – fear of trees

Emetophobia – fear of vomiting

Geliophobia – fear of laughter

Hexakosioihexekontahexaphobia – fear of the number 666

Iatrophobia – fear of doctors

Lachanophobia – fear of vegetables

Neophobia – fear of anything new

Octophobia – fear of the number eight

Odontophobia – fear of teeth or dentists

Pantophobia – fear of everything

Phasmophobia – fear of ghosts

Pogonophobia – fear of beards

Pteronophobia – fear of being tickled by feathers

Scoleciphobia – fear of worms

Scolionophobia – fear of school

Syngenesophobia – fear of relatives

Triskaidekaphobia – fear of the number 13

Xenophobia – fear of strangers or foreigners

The following people suffered/suffer from the fears in brackets after their names:

Actor Johnny Depp (clowns)

Queen Elizabeth I (roses)

Singer Madonna (thunder)

Actress Joan Collins (the dark)

Actress Natalie Wood (water – ironically, she died by drowning)

Singer Prince (heights and dirt)

Actor Sir Sean Connery (needles)

Film director Sir Alfred Hitchcock (policemen – he refused to learn to drive for fear of being stopped by a policeman)

Singer Christina Aguilera (the dark – she sleeps with the light on)

Singer Rachel Stevens (locked toilet doors)

Actor Robert De Niro (dentists)

TV presenter Ant McPartlin (spiders)

Julius Caesar (cats)

Actress Julia Roberts (spiders)

Actor Ross Kemp (snakes)

Actress Angela Griffin (injections)

TV presenter Claudia Winkleman (spiders)

Comedian Jenny Eclair (fish – live ones, not on a plate)

Actor Leonardo DiCaprio (Needles)

Comedian Lee Evans (the colour green – he once freaked out when he was made to wear a green suit)

Actress and singer Barbra Streisand (public toilets: she often travels in a fully equipped Winnebago so she never has to sit on a public toilet seat: she also scatters rose petals in the toilet bowl before using it).)

Actress Rachel Weisz (Frogs – she's been known to go without a bath rather than evict amphibian intruders from her ground-floor bathroom)

Actor George Clooney (earthquakes)

Rapper Eminem (owls)

Actress Reese Witherspoon (spiders)

Actor Billy Bob Thornton (antiques and clowns)

Actress Kate Beckinsale (throwing up)

Actor Tobey Maguire (spiders – ironically since he is probably most famous for playing Spider-Man in the film of the same name!)

Actor Matthew McConaughey (revolving doors and tunnels)

Actress Nicole Kidman (butterflies)

Actor and singer Justin Timberlake (spiders)

TV presenter Declan Donnelly (pigeons)

Actress Jennifer Aniston (flying)

ENGROSSING BACTERIA

Although I've called them 'gross', most bacteria aren't. In fact, 95 per cent of bacteria are harmless or even beneficial. Some bacteria have adapted to survive at human body temperature and we get benefits from them that help to keep us alive – for instance, bacteria that help us digest our food. Sounds like a great relationship! This mutually beneficial system is called 'symbiosis'.

Unfortunately, it's the five per cent of bad, harmful bacteria that give the rest a bad name.

So, given that about 70 per cent of all living things in the world are bacteria, that's still an awful lot of bad bacteria.

Each gram of soil holds more than a billion bacteria.

There are more bacteria in your mouth than there are people in the world.

Every square inch of a light switch has 200 bacteria on it.

Bacteria reproduce by splitting in half. Therefore, in a matter of hours, one bacterium can become one billion bacteria.

Your sponge contains more bacteria than your toilet.

The heat from headphones causes 700 times more bacteria than normal to grow in the ears.

Every square centimetre of the human body has an average of 13 million bacteria on it.

According to a study that took swabs from everyday objects and analysed them for bacteria, mobile phones are worse than door handles and computer keyboards. Our mobiles are also worse than the bottoms of our shoes and even worse than toilet seats.

A professor of microbiology has explained what makes mobile phones worse than (almost) anything else. The clue is in the name. Being 'mobile', they are stored in bags or pockets, are handled frequently, and held close to the face. In other words, they come into contact with more parts of our body and a wider range of bacteria than toilet seats! The phones contained more skin bacteria than any other object; this could be due to the fact that this type of bacteria increases in high temperatures and our phones are perfect for breeding these germs as they're kept warm and cosy in our pockets, handbags and briefcases. These bacteria are toxic to humans, and can cause infections if they have the opportunity to enter the body.

We have been warned . . . let's all go and clean our phones!

If your body's natural defences failed, the bacteria in your gut would consume you within 48 hours, eating you from the inside out.

ENGROSSING SWEAT

Why do we sweat? Basically, our bodies work best when we are about 37 degrees Celsius, but in hot weather or hot rooms or if we exercise or dress too warmly, we heat up higher than that. If that continued, we wouldn't be able to tolerate heat and our bodies would eventually explode from over-heating.

Luckily, the body has ways to deal with overheating. A part of your brain called the hypothalamus helps control temperature. When you start to get too hot, it sends an urgent message to sweat glands – of which there are millions all over our bodies – to start making sweat (also known as perspiration). This leaves your skin through tiny holes called pores. Sweat is made of water, salt and sugar. When it hits the air, it starts to evaporate (this means it turns from a liquid to a vapour). As the sweat evaporates off your skin, you cool down.

Sweat is a great cooling system, but if you're

sweating a lot on a hot day, or after playing hard, you could be losing too much water through your skin. Then you need to put liquid back in your body by drinking plenty of water so you don't get dehydrated.

Sweat by itself doesn't smell at all. It's the bacteria that live on your skin that mix with the sweat and give it a stinky smell. So it's stale sweat – rather than sweat itself – that smells. And sweaty unwashed clothes can really honk! Fortunately, regular washing with soap and water keeps most of us fresh and nice to be near. However, when you reach puberty, special hormones affect the glands in your armpits, and these glands make some individuals smellier than others: these people may need a gentle hint to wash more, or use products that will help them become nicer to be around.

Men usually have much more active sweat glands than women.

You don't sweat evenly under each arm. Right-handed people sweat more under their left arm while left-handers get sweatier under their right arm.

Due to the lack of a particular enzyme that absorbs a smelly protein made by bacteria in the stomach, some people's bodies give off a ghastly rotten-fish odour in their sweat.

An average pair of feet has half a million sweat glands, and these can produce half a litre of perspiration a day. A lot of this sweat comes from between our toes. Athlete's foot is a condition caused by a fungus dining on the fatty acids in the sweat that pours out of the pores in the skin between our toes. It's also known as 'toe-jam' (yeughh!).

Interestingly, the sweat that oozes from our pores is actually a weak version of pee, made up of the same components: water, salts and urea.

Human sweat contains a chemical that is the same as wasp poison.

Sweat glands are little coiled-up tubes. If you stretched out and lined up all the sweat glands in one human end to end, the line would be over 2,000 miles long.

ENGROSSING
VOMIT

Sorry. This was a really good picture but I was sick on it

When something upsets your stomach and your body knows it has to get rid of it, a button is pushed in a part of your brain called 'the emetic centre'. This then rejects the stomach's contents so you vomit! The mushy, part-digested food or liquid in your stomach gets mixed with saliva, or *spit,* and acidic stomach juices (which give vomit its characteristic smell*), and comes back up your throat and out of your mouth.

It is, as you probably know yourself, a ghastly experience.

So much so that there are lots of words in the English language to describe it – from emesis (the posh one), to puking, barfing, chucking up, chundering – even 'bowling it' for those who are forced to sit with their heads over the toilet bowl.

Sometimes it tastes like the food you just ate – or something a lot worse – and it's usually the same colour as what you last ate. Too much chocolate will look brown and yucky, while an overdose of chips and tomato ketchup will look orange.

Some foods, such as root vegetables and corn

---

*Specifically hydrochloric acid, which is so strong that it can go through stainless steel and eat through paint.

kernels, take a lot longer for the stomach's acids to break down and digest, so even if you haven't just eaten carrots, swede or parsnips, they may be more obviously noticeable than the more easily digestible foods which have formed a general mush.

Lazzaro Spallanzani was an 18th-century Italian scientist who was famous for discovering that bats use sound to navigate, but we're much more interested in his work on digestion. In his *Dissertationi di fisica animale e vegetale* (two vols, 1780), he established that we don't grind down food in our stomachs (as was previously thought) but dissolve it in chemicals. Not to put too fine a point on it, Lazzaro was just fascinated by barfing and so he decided to . . . wait for it . . . prepare to look away if you've just eaten . . . no, really, I mean it . . . all right, don't say I didn't warn you . . . here it comes . . . he decided to *eat his own vomit*! But that wasn't enough for the good professor. Oh no, he decided to puke up this vomit (fair enough) and *then eat it again*! If that doesn't have you screaming 'URGH!' then nothing ever will. But wait a minute . . . he then proceeded to puke it up a third time and eat it again.

That is what you call real dedication to science. Either that or he just liked the taste of barf!

New Year's Eve is a date in the calendar that's big on vomit. Which is why on one New Year's Eve, vomit vigilantes (called 'Clean Teams') were sent to New York city's Grand Central Station.

They were supposed to thrust a bag under the chin of anyone who seemed about to throw up.

The record for projectile vomiting is eight metres. That's one record that not many people will want to beat . . .

Scary rides in amusement parks cause a lot of people to vomit. This can actually be dangerous as the centrifugal forces can send the vomit back down a person's throat and prevent them from breathing.

If you're about to vomit but can't bear the thought of it, there's no point in closing your mouth: if you really have to vomit, it will come up whether you want it to or not. If you were really able to keep your mouth closed, then it would come out of your nose instead.

ENGROSSING NOSES AND SMELLS

Thanks to the miracle of publishing*, we know that eating your own bogeys isn't that bad for you. This being the case, it is extraordinary that, according to the statistics, only three per cent of people eat their own bogeys.

Why Eating Bogeys is Good For You (by Mitchell Symons). Available in all good bookshops, etc., etc.

Personally, I don't trust those statistics because I am a bogey-muncher, and so are most people I know (well, I've caught quite a few in my time, I can tell you!). And then there's that old joke – *What's the difference between cabbage and bogeys? Answer: You can't get a kid to eat cabbage . . .*

However, if those figures are accurate, it means that 97 per cent of nose-pickers are parking their bogeys somewhere other than in their gobs. And given that there are an awful lot of rhinotillexomaniacs (nose-pickers) out there, there must be bucket-loads of bogeys dotted all over the place.

Now THAT is gross.

In a survey of nose-pickers, only 2.1 per cent admitted that they did it for enjoyment. Only 2.1 per cent? I don't believe it! So now, not only am I one of the three per cent of bogey-munchers I'm also one of the 2.1 per cent of recreational pickers. Mind you, you'd think there'd be a huge crossover between the two groups.

Most respondents to the survey said they only picked their noses 'to relieve discomfort or itchiness'. Well, aren't they the saints!

There are sugars in bogeys – and that's probably what makes them so irresistible to us bogey-eaters. Or should I say 'mucophagics' – as mucophagy is the medical term for the consumption of the nasal mucus obtained from nose picking.

According to something I found on the internet (so be aware that it might not be 100 per cent accurate), the average person can fit their little finger up one side of their nostrils. If they stick both little fingers in at the same time, then only one-quarter (as opposed to the one-half you presumably might have expected) of each little finger fits.

No, I'm not overwhelmed by this either, but here's the thing: the first thing I did after reading this was to stick my little fingers up my hooter – and I'm pretty sure you did EXACTLY the same too. So what I suggest is that you read this out to your parents or your teacher or some other adult – or perhaps just leave the book open at this page – and then pretend to leave the room. Once they think you're out of sight, I bet you that they too have a good old rummage around their noses. Pick that moment to walk back into the room!

One in three male motorists picks his nose while driving. Yup, that's me, one in three.

Sometimes it's hard to remember that noses aren't just for picking but for sneezing too.

Sneezes come out of our noses at speeds of up to 160 kilometres per hour. That's probably why it's impossible to keep your eyes open when you sneeze (be my guest and have a go, but you really won't be able to do it!). The velocity of sneezes is as good a reason as any to cover your nose and mouth when you sneeze. The same applies to coughs (although these 'only' travel at 100 kilometres per hour – a similar speed to laughs).

People who live in the city have longer, thicker nose hairs than people who live in the country (because they breathe more polluted air).

The San Blas women of Panama consider giant noses a mark of great beauty. They paint black lines down the centre of their noses to make them appear longer.

Different smells appeal to different people. The Dogon people of Africa use fried onions as a perfume. They rub them all over their body because they think the smell's so attractive.

Everyone   except for identical twins   has a unique smell. A newborn baby is able to recognize its mother's smell, and many of us can recognize the smell of people we know well. Obviously, that smell might just be a perfume or after-shave they use regularly, but smells are also determined by genetics, by environment and by diet – all of them combining to make a unique smell for every person.

The average smell weighs 760 nanograms.

Astronauts lose their sense of smell in space because there is no gravity to move smells around. It also means that the fluid in their sinuses doesn't drain away automatically but remains there while they're on their missions. As for snoring, the word is that if they snore on earth – they snore in space too!

While we're on the subject of smells, a survey published in the French newspaper *Le Figaro* reported that the French wash less than other people. They also wash less than they claim to.

Girls can detect smells better than boys, and this superiority applies to females of all ages.

Studies have shown that women are better able than men to identify a smell. Two per cent of the population – male and female – have absolutely no sense of smell at all.

ENGROSSING LIGHTNING STRIKES

Lightning can – and does – kill. You don't even have to be in the middle of a storm to be struck, as lightning can strike 16 kilometres away from a storm.

If there's a lightning storm and your mum says, 'It's bath time,' or 'Come on, do the dishes,' it's the one time you might be permitted to refuse to obey, as lightning can strike through water taps – though it is extremely rare, and in modern, properly earthed houses, almost impossible. However, you're not allowed to go on the computer or watch TV either, as they're no less dangerous in a lightning storm! Mums take note . . .

You should also keep off the phone during storms because electricity can go from the phone through your ear and into your brain. Many people – including kids – have been injured while talking on the phone during storms.

If you're outside when lightning strikes, DON'T shelter under a tree. Instead, you should go into a building or a car (and don't forget to wind up the windows!). An oak tree is worse than (almost) any other kind of tree to shelter under in a storm. Why are oaks more dangerous? Their roots go deeper, which make a better electrical earth for the lightning.

Once every three or four days an American dies after being struck by lightning. Sounds scary, but then you have to remember that there are more than 300 million people living in the USA. If my maths are correct (and if they're not I'm sure you'll write in and tell me), this means that the risk of any Americans being killed by lightning in any given year is about one in three million. Assuming that those statistics hold for Britain too (and my instinct is that we're *less* susceptible to lightning deaths as we enjoy much milder weather), I'd happily take those odds. Even though . . .

. . . men are six times more likely to be struck by lightning than women.

Two-thirds of the people struck by lightning survive.

An average bolt of lightning is less than 1.5 cm thick and packs 30 million volts!

Thunderstorms can approach as fast as 50 miles an hour.

It's said that you are more likely to be infected by flesh-eating bacteria than you are to be struck by lightning and that, according to the proverb at least, lightning doesn't strike twice. Well, someone should have told American Roy Sullivan about that.

Sullivan was a park ranger in Virginia's Shenandoah National Park. Between 1942 and 1977 Sullivan was hit by lightning on no fewer than *seven* different occasions and – no less incredibly – he survived each time. As a result, he earned the nicknames the Human Lightning Conductor and the Human Lightning Rod, and was recognized by *The Guinness Book of World Records* as the person struck by lightning more recorded times than anyone else.

All these strikes were documented by the superintendent of Shenandoah National Park and were verified by doctors. Sullivan said that he'd been hit other times too – the first time as a child: he was helping his father to cut wheat in a field, when a bolt struck the blade of his scythe. However, because he didn't have any proof, he didn't ask for it to be added to his official tally.

You might guess that he died from the seventh and final strike but you'd be wrong. In fact, he shot himself in 1983 at the age of 71.

Anyway, here for the record are Sullivan's seven strikes.

Strike 1: 1942. He was hiding from a thunderstorm in a fire lookout tower that didn't have a lightning rod. The tower was hit seven or eight times, and so Sullivan ran out and received what he reckoned was his worst lightning strike, which burned a strip all along his right leg, hit his toe, and left a hole in his shoe.

Strike 2: 1969. After 27 years of being lightning free, Sullivan was entitled to think that those days were behind him . . . WRONG! He was hit while driving his truck on a mountain road. A vehicle's metal body normally protects people, but this time the lightning hit nearby trees and was deflected into the open window of the truck. The strike knocked Sullivan unconscious and burned off his eyebrows, eyelashes, and most of his hair. The out-of-control truck kept moving until it stopped near a cliff edge.

Strike 3: 1970. Sullivan was struck in his garden. The lightning hit a nearby power transformer and from there jumped to his left shoulder, searing it.

Strike 4: 1972. Sullivan was working inside the ranger station in Shenandoah National Park when a lightning strike set his hair on fire. At this point, he was starting to think he was jinxed and would be struck even if he were in a crowd of people.

Strike 5: 1973. By now, Sullivan was entitled to feel unlucky. Out on patrol in the park, he saw a storm cloud forming and drove away quickly. When he finally thought he had outrun it, he decided it was safe to leave his truck but was struck by a lightning bolt that he later said he actually saw hit him. The lightning set his hair on fire, moved down his left arm and left leg and crossed over to his right leg just below the knee. Still conscious, Sullivan crawled to his truck and poured a can of water, which he always kept there, over his head.

Strike 6: 1976. Sullivan was struck by a bolt of lightning that injured his ankle.

Strike 7: 1977. Sullivan was fishing when a lightning bolt hit the top of his head and travelled down, burning his chest and stomach.

ENGROSSING
CREATURES
AND US

On any one square centimetre of our skin there
are some eight million microscopic animals.

We even have microscopic mites living in our eyelashes.

More than 100 million microcreatures are living in your mouth at any one time.

Parasites count for 0.01 per cent of your body weight. So now my excuse for being overweight is that I'm carrying too many parasites . . . No, I didn't think anyone would believe it.

Tapeworms – more properly known as cestodes – are parasitic flatworms that live in the digestive tracts of many animals, including . . . *us*! They range in size from about 0.1 centimetres to more than 15 metres in length. The longest recorded tapeworm ever found in a human body was 33 metres long.

The foot is the part of the body most often bitten by insects.

Head lice are a common problem in the UK, especially among school children. Lice pass from one person to another during direct head-to-head contact. This is because lice cannot jump, fly or hop; they can only transfer to another head by walking along strands of hair. Children whispering secrets at school or families enjoying a cuddle at home provide head lice with the ideal opportunity to travel from one head to the next. Having said that, you CAN'T get lice from pillows or hats: it has to be from other people.

The head louse is a tiny greyish-brown insect, about 2.5 millimetres long. Head lice cling to hair and are usually found near the scalp. They live on blood from the host, which they get by biting through the skin. The adult lice mate. The female then lays eggs that are firmly attached to hair close to the scalp and can be very difficult to remove. After a week or so, the baby louse hatches out of the egg, leaving behind a shiny white empty eggshell on a strand of hair.

It is commonly – but wrongly – thought that you get head lice from poor hygiene (i.e. from not washing). In fact, lice are equally likely to be found on clean hair as on dirty hair. Interestingly, though, they don't seem to like the smell/taste of chlorine – so that's a great excuse for not washing your hair after swimming.

Identical twins have 100 per cent identical DNA.

We share our DNA with other people/things to the following extent:

99.9 per cent with every other human being

98.4 per cent with chimpanzees

92 per cent with dolphins

90 per cent with other mammals

70 per cent with slugs

44 per cent with fruit flies

26 per cent with yeast

18 per cent with lettuce

Please note that the above list should be treated with plenty of suspicion. That's not because I didn't do any checking but, rather, because I did. There was no doubt about the amount of DNA we share with twins, people and chimpanzees. It was while I was travelling down the food chain (so to speak) that problems started to emerge. Take lettuce, for example. The extraordinary fact is that we share *any* DNA with lettuce. So whether it's 33 per cent, as I saw claimed in some book (oops, it was one of mine) or 15 per cent (as I've also seen) or the 18 per cent I decided to go with here, doesn't seem to me to actually matter very much. The fact that, when it comes to dressing myself, I must now consider oil and vinegar as suitable, is quite startling enough for me.

Creepy crawlies can be beneficial to humans – and not just because of their role in the ecosystem. They can actually be used in medicine.

In the old days, maggots would be put in soldiers' wounds because doctors realized that maggots were only interested in eating dead tissue, and left healthy new living tissue alone. So they were really useful for cleaning up infected wounds. There was also an additional benefit: while munching on all the decayed flesh, the maggots also released a kind of antibiotic that helped to cleanse the wound – often saving people from dying of gangrene.

But we're not just talking about the past! Even today, creepy crawlies are put to medical use. As you probably know, leeches feed on blood. In doing so, they inject an anti-coagulant (a substance that stops blood from clotting) so they can suck it up for longer. This is so effective that doctors in the UK still sometimes use leeches when they want to prevent clotting.

Every year the average person eats 428 bugs by mistake. But, fortunately, many of those are quite tiny. What isn't true – even though I used to think it was! – is that the average person will swallow eight spiders in their sleep during a lifetime. Phew!

In Somalia, sheep fat is used to treat a variety of ailments, from rheumatism to broken bones and chest pains.

Until 2009, residents of Talkeetna, Alaska, held an annual Moose Dropping Festival, in which jewellery was made out of moose dung and swizzle sticks were decorated with – yes, you guessed it – moose poo. Then there were the 750 gold-painted moose turds that were

individually numbered and dropped out of a helium balloon onto a field on which a giant X was painted. The gold-painted moose turd that landed closest to the X won its 'owner' $1,000. It all sounds great fun, but after 37 years the Talkeetna Historical Society announced the cancellation of the festival. Don't ask me why: I don't make the rules, I just report on them.

Pearlescent lipstick used to contain fish scales. The shimmering effects were made using a substance called 'pearlescence' found in the scales.

Perfume is frequently made from – among other things – a waxy, musky substance called ambergris, which is pooed out or vomited up by certain species of whale. So the next time you smell someone's perfume, try not to think of whale sick!

The dog might be man's best friend, but try telling that to the pooches that bite us. According to hospital figures, one in 350 people gets bitten by dogs every year.

On the other hand, nearly two-thirds of dog

owners admit to kissing their dogs. Of these, some 45 per cent kissed them on the nose, 19 per cent on the neck, seven per cent on the back, five per cent on the stomach and two per cent on the legs. An additional 29 per cent listed the place they kiss their dog as 'other'!

It is estimated that people fear spiders more than they do death but, in fact, you are statistically more likely to be killed by a champagne cork than by a poisonous spider.

Every year, more people worldwide are killed by donkeys than are killed in plane crashes. Strangely, I take little comfort from this fact as I fly much more often than I ride donkeys.

In the USA nine milligrams of rat droppings are allowed in a kilogram of wheat.

Polar bear liver contains so much vitamin A that it could be fatal to a human if eaten.

Men from the Dassanech tribe of Ethiopia daub their bodies with cow dung.

Although humans are not their regular or typical prey, tigers have killed more people than any other cat. Between 1800 and 1900, tigers killed over 300,000 people in India alone.

Every year, the public parks of London are sprayed with more than three million litres of dog wee.

ENGROSSING LIVING

Although I'm not a teetotaller (someone who NEVER drinks alcohol), my alcoholic intake is so tiny that I might as well be. This is not to show off what a splendid man I am: I just don't like the effects of alcohol and, when it comes to over-indulgence, I'd much rather compensate with chocolate. In fact, research has shown alcohol – in moderation – to be beneficial. However, the key word there is 'moderation'. Too much alcohol consumption is one of the biggest problems in our society. Specifically, alcohol abuse is linked to:

65 per cent of suicide attempts

76,000 facial injuries a year

23 per cent of child neglect calls to national helplines

39 per cent of fires

15 per cent of drownings

In a contest held by a British magazine to try to discover who had the worst boss, many people agreed with the statement that their boss could be replaced by a hamster and no one would notice.

10 per cent of British adults admit to wearing the same item of underwear three days in a row.

More than three billion people in the world are malnourished – that's to say they don't have enough food. This is the highest number (and proportion) of hungry people ever recorded in history.

In a survey it was discovered that half of all homes surveyed had 'faecal material' (that's poo to you and me) in their washing machines, and underwear contained as much as 10 grams of faecal matter. Washing doesn't always get rid of this f.m. because people wash lots of clothes together – thereby spreading the faecal contamination around. Yeughh!

As for faecal material in hotels, a survey found that – surprise, surprise – there was more of the disgusting stuff in cheap hotel rooms than in expensive ones.

Having work done to your home? It's reckoned that, in your lifetime, you will have 22 workmen examine the (dirty) contents of your linen basket.

At a wedding reception you have a one-in-a-hundred chance of catching a cold sore from one of the other guests.

A quarter of adolescent men don't use a deodorant.

Young children are poisoned by houseplants more often than they are by detergents or other chemicals.

According to Dr Charles Gerba, an American microbiologist who calls himself the 'Sultan of Slime', in the average home, the toilet is cleaner then the kitchen. This is not because toilets are especially clean, but because people are more careful about cleaning them than they are their kitchens. He says that the kitchen nasties include dishcloths, cutting boards, sponges and taps, and that the floor is often cleaner than the sink! Dr Gerba is also the man who 'discovered' that a toilet sprays droplets of its contents when it is flushed. He used a strobe light to shoot a time-lapse photograph of a flush and captured the evidence. So always put the lid down before you flush!

In case you've ever wondered, the chances of being injured by a toilet seat at some point in your lifetime are one in 6,500.

Have you ever seen the classic silent film *The Gold Rush*? There's a wonderful scene in it in which Charlie Chaplin is so hungry that he eats his shoes (complete with spaghetti laces). In fact, leather shoes do have some nutrition – albeit only a tiny amount. So if you were starving to death, you could survive for a little bit longer if you ate your shoes.

In a book entitled *Civilization and Its Discontents*, Sigmund Freud wrote that civilization only became possible when men resisted the urge to put out their camp fires by peeing on them. In other words, they had to be able to look into the future and realize that they would want a fire the next day rather than only satisfying the short-term urge to pee on a fire.

Your body gives off enough heat in half an hour to bring a litre of water to the boil.

Your ears secrete more earwax when you're afraid than when you're relaxed.

You know that feeling you get when you read or see something truly yucky? That's *disgust* (or at least it should be!). Disgust is an important human reaction as it protects us from things that are harmful to us.

The disgust reaction is thought to have evolved to help us to avoid illness. For example, our disgust at other people's bodily excretions and secretions helps us to avoid them and their diseases.

Women feel disgust more than men do – probably because historically they have had to protect both themselves and their children from disease.

Disgust works across the senses – whether it's the sound of someone vomiting, or the sight of pus – and it's common in all cultures.

Doctors from the London School of Hygiene and Tropical Medicine conducted an experiment in which 40,000 people were asked to look at pictures, including body lesions, poo, rotting meat and parasites. Pictures featuring objects associated with disease (like a bloody towel) were voted more disgusting than pictures featuring objects *not* associated with disease (like a towel with a blue stain).

ENGROSSING DYING

When you die, your hair and nails continue to grow for a while.

On average, murderers are 7.5 years younger than their victims.

There have been more deaths of Americans in car accidents than in ALL the wars in which the USA has fought since independence (1776).

On average, one American drowns in their own bath EVERY day. More Americans, however, simply freeze to death (just under twice as many). Much worse, 35 Americans die every day from falls.

Children have been known to drown in toilets.

There is only one person in all recorded history who has been killed by a meteorite. A man named Manfredo Settala from Milan in Italy in 1680. Mind you, he was 80 at the time!

People have died after shaking vending machines that have then fallen on top of them.

How do doctors know for certain that someone is dead? Nowadays, there are machines that can test for brain activity, but what if a machine isn't available? In that case, there are other (hopefully!) reliable methods which include:

• pouring freezing water in the person's ear

• poking something in their eye

• poking something down their throat

• grinding knuckles into the base of their spine

Oh well, it's better to be safe than sorry, and we wouldn't want a return to the 1500s, when one out of every 25 coffins was found to have scratch marks on the inside.

The ashes of a cremated person weigh an average of four kilograms. A big part of our body weight is the water trapped in our cells. When people are cremated, not only are all the bones and tissues burned, but all that water evaporates, leaving very little behind.

For those people who prefer to be buried, there is the pretty grisly certainty of their corpses being chewed by insects. Still, undertakers take great care to preserve their 'clients' for as long as possible. To stop insects entering the corpse via the nose, they pack it with cotton wool laced with a liquid insecticide.

Nowadays, undertakers are much more likely to select the right coffin. There was a time – not so long ago (before the 1940s) – when, if a body didn't fit into a coffin, the undertaker would break the corpse's ankles and bend back the feet.

The death cap is the world's most poisonous mushroom. It actually contains five different types of poison, which cause damage to internal organs, resulting in coma and death.

The human brain continues sending out electrical wave signals for up to 36 hours following death. That sounds OK, but what *doesn't* is this: the human brain remains conscious for about 15 seconds after a person has been decapitated. This is because there is still blood in the head. How horrible is that?

Monday is the day of the week when the risk of a fatal heart attack is greatest. A 10-year Scottish study found that 20 per cent more people die of heart attacks on Mondays than on any other day of the week. It's thought to be due to a combination of too much fun over the weekend and the stress of going back to work.

Performers – especially comedians – sometimes talk about 'dying on stage' when a performance has gone particularly badly. Well, here are some

people who really *did* die on stage . . .

Tommy Cooper: Extremely popular comedian and magician whose act consisted of deliberately getting tricks wrong (and occasionally 'surprising' himself when they went right). He collapsed on stage during a live TV performance in 1984. The audience thought it was part of his act and laughed – until everyone realized it was serious.

Sid James: The actor who starred in the *Carry On* films. He had a heart attack while acting in *The Mating Season* at the Sunderland Empire Theatre in 1976. An announcer called for the curtain to close and requested a doctor. Again, the audience laughed, believing the events to be part of the show. Sid James was taken to hospital by ambulance, but died about an hour later.

Leonard Rossiter: Another great comic actor (*Rising Damp, Reginald Perrin*, etc.),he died while waiting to go on stage at London's Lyric Theatre in 1984.

Richard Versalle: The opera singer was performing at New York's Metropolitan Opera in 1996. The role required him to climb a six-metre ladder but, as he did so, he suffered a heart attack and fell to the stage, dead – just after singing the line 'Too bad you can only live so long'.

Leonard Warren: Another opera singer. He also died on stage at New York's Metropolitan Opera, but 36 years earlier in 1960. He had just completed an aria (operatic song) which began with the words 'To die, a momentous thing,' when he stopped singing and fell face-down on to the floor, remaining motionless. A few minutes later he was pronounced dead (from a massive cerebral haemorrhage – or stroke) and the rest of the performance was cancelled.

Sylvia Syms: An American jazz singer. She died on stage at the Algonquin Hotel in New York City in 1992 from a heart attack.

Here are some famous people with a twin who died at birth – or very soon after

Singer Elvis Presley

Actor Sir David Jason (didn't discover this until he was 14)

Writer Edgar Allan Poe

Artist Leonardo da Vinci

Writer Lewis Carroll

Writer Oscar Wilde

Singer and actor Justin Timberlake

Actor Jim Broadbent

N.B. Andy Garcia was born with a partly formed twin on his shoulder.

Here is a list of people whose organs were preserved after death – along with the organ!

Scientist Albert Einstein's brain

Poet Percy Bysshe Shelley's heart

Astronomer Galileo's finger

Russian revolutionary Vladimir Lenin's brain

Composer Joseph Haydn's head

Explorer Dr David Livingstone's heart

President George Washington's tooth

King Richard II's jawbone

Writer Thomas Hardy's heart

ENGROSSING POO AND PEE

You produce 200 grams of poo each day –
on average, but more if you eat more (and,
unsurprisingly, less if you eat less).

Healthy human poo is three-quarters water. If it's less, then you might be suffering from constipation – which means you have difficulty in pooing. If your poo has too much water, then you've probably got diarrhoea – an upset tummy, perhaps caused by eating something bad.

About a 10th of our poo contains nutrients useful to other creatures – which is why they eat our poo if they get the chance.

A full bladder is a bit larger than a cricket or tennis ball. The average bladder holds 400–600 millilitres of fluid, but can actually hold *double* this amount without rupturing if it has to (e.g. if there's something wrong with you and you simply can't pee). In any event, you should never hold onto your pee when your bladder is so full that you run the risk of it rupturing or the pee backing up into the kidneys. There is a story of a woman who was so absorbed in playing on her Nintendo Wii (yes, I do see the pun) that she didn't go to the loo and eventually died from the consequences of a ruptured bladder.

Fortunately, holding on for that long shouldn't be a problem as most people feel the need to pee when their bladder's half full (i.e. when it's holding 200–300 millilitres). At the point when you're *really* bursting to go, your bladder probably still isn't even full!

According to a survey, 28 per cent of people admit to peeing in a swimming pool. That is so gross, but even grosser is when people *poo* in a pool. We were once on holiday in western France and we went to an artificial lake that had been designed as a swimming pool. As I was swimming with my sons, I noticed a huge – and I do mean *huge* – log floating past us. On closer inspection, I was horrified to discover that it wasn't a log but a gigantic turd. I don't think I've ever got out of a pool so quickly in my life!

Most people hold their breath when they start peeing.

Eating beetroot can turn your pee red.

Vitamin B2 can turn it bright yellow.

Certain blue dyes (typically found in cheap sweets) can turn it blue-green.

Rhubarb can turn it slightly pink.

Drinking turpentine – the stuff you use to clean paintbrushes – is said to make pee smell like roses. Which is why, years ago, women drank turpentine. I strongly advise you NOT to attempt to revive this strange and extremely harmful practice.

The Germans take a great interest in their poo. That's why, traditionally, a German toilet had a sort of shelf above the water so that people could inspect their poo. It turns out that this interest in poo has also, in times gone by, extended to other people's poo. In rural Germany, people used to display their poo in their front gardens. The more poo you had on show, the wealthier (and therefore

more important) you were considered by the neighbours. It sounds disgusting but there's something in it (no, I don't mean 'in the poo'). The wealthier you were, the more food you could eat and therefore the more poo you would produce! Nowadays, people use cars instead of poo as status symbols. Ideally, there wouldn't be any need for status symbols but if you must have them, then I suppose a flash car trumps last night's supper.

The American people produce about 5,500 kilograms of poo per second. Their livestock (cattle, pigs, sheep, etc.) produce more than 110,000 kilograms of poo per second.

The germs present in human faeces can pass through up to 10 layers of toilet paper. And, no, that's NOT an encouragement to you to use 10 sheets of toilet paper at a time!

If only all these germs – including over 120 different viruses – would all stay in the loo, the world would be a lot better place. Alas, because so many people's personal hygiene habits are so poor, germs from poo – especially *Escherichia coli* – are found everywhere. Just to give you an example: traces of the *E. coli* bacterium were found on 10 per cent of mugs in American coffee shops.

If you had a choice of washing in your own spit or your own pee, you should opt for the pee (not that it's much of a choice, I grant you). Fresh pee is more sterile than spit. Healthy pee isn't home to bacteria.

The French use less toilet paper (around four kilograms per person per year) than any other European people; the Swedes use the most (over eight kilograms), while the British are sixth in the European loo-roll table, with four and a half kilograms. In total we use nearly 1.5 billion loo rolls, more than 200,000 tons, a year.

As regular readers will know, poo gets its distinct brown colour from the mixture of dead red blood cells (or haemoglobin) that we're constantly shedding and the bile that comes out of the liver and gall bladder. Newborn babies don't have much in the way of dead red blood cells, and that's why their poo is green – especially in the first few evacuations (see below).

Foods with a very high fibre content – like sweetcorn and seeds – sometimes pass through our bodies without getting digested.

The average person will spend some six months of their lives on the toilet . . . but not necessarily in one go.

The percentage of men who wash their hands after using the toilet is 55 per cent. The percentage of women who wash their hands after using the toilet is 80 per cent. Here's a fascinating fact to consider: a study found that *three* times as many people claimed to have washed their hands after going to the toilet than had actually done so.

Babies pee and sometimes poo in their mothers' stomachs. Yes they do. But it's not quite as dreadful as it sounds. The wee doesn't contain the same waste as ordinary pee, and nor is it yellow. The pooing is actually quite rare, but foetuses (babies in the womb) do accumulate a sort of green poo called meconium. They only rarely pass any of this in the womb: most wait until they've been born. Unlike our poo, this green stuff isn't dirty and it doesn't smell, but it's not particularly nice to look at when it appears in a newborn baby's very first nappy.

Some 45.2 per cent of people admit to peeing in the shower while 44.9 per cent of people admit to peeing in the sea.

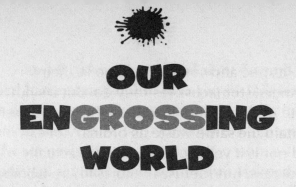

OUR ENGROSSING WORLD

Ethyl mercaptan is one of the smelliest things in the world, and that's why it's often added to the (otherwise odourless) gas we have piped into our homes so that we can easily detect a gas leak.

Newborn babies are given to the wrong mother 12 times a day in maternity wards across the world.

According to a Canadian researcher, left-handed people are more accident-prone than right-handers and are likely to die younger. The researcher looked at the records of over 2,000 ex-professional baseball players and discovered that left-handers over the age of 35 were two per cent more likely to die than right-handers of the same age. Worse news (for us lefties): there were very few left-handers in the group who made it beyond 85 years old. In another Canadian study of left-handers (they've certainly

got time on their hands in Canada), it was
found that 44 per cent of left-handers had been
hospitalized within the last five years due to an
accident – compared to just 36 per cent of the
right-handers. The reason usually given for why
left-handers fare so relatively badly is that the
tools and machines of our modern world are
designed for right-handers. Sounds about right.

If you are involved in a car accident, your
chances of getting hurt are only one in 10. If
you have an accident on a motorcycle, it's the
other way around. Your chances of getting hurt
are nine in 10.

The Mediterranean is the world's most polluted
sea – with untreated sewage washing in from
over 100 European cities. It doesn't surprise me
as I've long found the Med to be an absolute
cesspool, totally unsuitable for bathing. What
I could never understand, as I sat on the beach
on the French Côte d'Azur gazing at the filthy
water, is how they managed to fly the blue EU
flag that denotes a clean beach. One day it was
all explained to me by a local. Unlike in the
UK, where the blue flag scheme is operated
scrupulously, in southern France, the local mafia

find out when the sea is due to be inspected and then pressurize all the local towns and businesses to refrain from dumping waste into the sea until *after* the inspection. That way, the EU inspector tests only clean water. I'm not sure I believed this local man (it's possible he had an axe to grind against criminals in the region), but it is at least an explanation for something that is otherwise inexplicable!

According to the National Safety Council, bicycles are the most dangerous objects in a typical home. Next on the list are stairs, then doors.

Disposable nappies make up 30 per cent of all the non-biodegradable rubbish buried in American landfills.

On 2 November, Haitians celebrate the 'Day of the Dead'. Followers visit the tombstones of relatives and pay their respects to Baron Samedi, the god of the dead. To show they are 'possessed' by spirits of the dead, followers often rub hot pepper juice on their bodies. Some hold swearing contests near the gates of the capital's large municipal cemetery. I don't like the idea of hot pepper juice on my body but I think I'd do pretty well in a swearing contest!

An American man was shot with a nail gun at work. The accident left him with a nine-centimetre nail embedded in his head. Incredibly, he was physically unharmed but the injury lowered his ability to do maths.

ENGROSSING FARTS

Less than one per cent of a fart is made up of the stinky stuff, but that's smelly enough to make it unpleasant. Put it this way: you can smell a fart in one part (however you measure it) in a million.

Farts are mostly created mostly by bacteria microfarting inside you.

Recently, there was an 11-year-old who farted 217 times in five minutes on a radio call-in show. His parents must have been *so* proud . . .

Women fart three times more often than men but are much better at disguising it. Men, on the other hand, are much more likely to boast about their farting 'skills'. A serious study on the differences between the sexes when it comes to farting found that, when fed exactly the same food, women produce more concentrated gas than men – in other words, they produced 'a greater odour intensity'.

It is known that gas escaping from a corpse can make it sound as if someone is farting after death. One man wrote to *Bizarre* magazine (clue's in the title, I guess) to say that he's eating lots of fruit and vegetables so he can go out with a bang when he dies. He added that his mother, a nurse, said that skinny people made the loudest farts.

The average fart releases 100 grams of gas – or should I say 'gases', as farts contain plenty of gases, including carbon dioxide and methane, which both contribute to global warming.

Farts have been clocked at speeds of three metres per second.

The most famous farter of all time was Le Pétomane (French for 'fart maniac'), a Frenchman whose real name was Joseph Pujol. Originally a baker, he used to entertain his customers by imitating musical instruments by farting. He took to the stage and adopted his new name. His act was phenomenally successful in Paris towards the end of the 19th century, with his highlights including the sound effects of cannon fire and thunderstorms, as well as playing 'O Sole Mio' and 'La Marseillaise' on an ocarina (an ancient flute-like 'wind' instrument) through a rubber tube connected to his bottom. He could also blow out a candle from a distance of several metres. He even farted his impression of the 1906 San Francisco earthquake.

Later in life, he retired from performing and returned to the bakery, opening a biscuit factory. He died in 1945, aged 88, and was buried in the cemetery of La Valette-du-Var, where his grave can still be seen today. The Sorbonne university offered his family a large sum of money to study his body after his death, but the family refused the offer.

Le Pétomane has a modern successor in a British 'flatulist' named Paul Oldfield who goes by the stage name Mr Methane and claims to be the only performing professional flatulist in the world. His 'rectal rumblings' include playing the British national anthem. On New Year's Eve he farts the countdown to midnight and then performs 'Auld Lang Syne'.

If you go to Mr Methane's own website – www. mrmethane.com/ – and there are worse things to do with your time – then you can read all about his extraordinary career.

The story of an unintentional flatulist was reported in *Scientific American* a few years ago. A 24-year-old man went to a hospital in Wales complaining of weird crackling sounds coming from pockets of air trapped under his skin. The sounds came from all over his body, including his bottom, providing a 'built-in whoopee-cushion effect'. It turns out that he had inflated a large number of balloons for a party earlier that day. His vigorous blowing had obviously caused this extraordinary effect.

The Yanomami, a tribe in South America, use farting as a greeting.

Flatulence runs in families, because they have a genetic tendency to harbour similar intestinal parasites as well as an inclination to eat the same types of foods.

A burp is not all that different from a fart – which is probably why some people call farts 'bottom burps'! We burp because when we eat or drink, we don't just swallow food or liquid, we also swallow air at the same time. That's where burping comes in. Excess gas is forced out of the stomach, up through the oesophagus (the tube that connects the back of the throat to the stomach), and then it emerges from the mouth as a burp.

The average person burps 15 times a day and farts 14 times a day. Guess I'm above average then . . .

If you farted continuously for six years and nine months, enough wind would be produced to equal the energy of an atomic bomb.

OH THAT'S TOO
GROSS!

In 1967 there was a medical case of a man with 12,568 boils on his body. No part of his skin was left uncovered by boils. The largest boil measured was nine centimetres in diameter. That's only three centimetres smaller than a CD.

In 1981 a man named Mr Bedlow consumed 5.8 kilograms of earwax. His target was six kilograms but he puked it all up before he could succeed. I went to school with a fellow of that name: I do hope it wasn't him!

A railroad worker named Phineas P. Gage was working with some dynamite that exploded unexpectedly. A metre-long iron bar weighing six kilograms went straight through his brain. He remained conscious, but couldn't see out of his left eye. After a while his sight returned and he fully recovered, although many people who knew him said that his personality changed and he became lazy and irritable. Mind you, he was entitled to, wasn't he?

A man named Henry Williamson refused to do a poo for eight months and 16 days (who knows why?). That's almost the duration of a human pregnancy. And when he finally did move his bowels, it must have really felt like giving birth.

People who work in mortuaries have to stroke the stomachs of dead people to help any gas remaining in their stomachs to escape. Well, you don't want people farting or burping from their coffins during their funerals.

Almost 90 per cent of people who consistently dye their hair develop eye cataracts because of a chemical in the dye called paraphenylenediamine.

The youngest parents on record are a Chinese couple, who gave birth to a normal boy when the father was nine years old and the mother was eight.

Occasionally people are born with horns. The majority of these horns protrude from people's foreheads, but some people have had horns on their thighs, backs, noses and feet.

A student at Rugby School managed to pop a spot and spray pus over a distance of two metres.

A teenager in India has an unusual party trick. He can drink milk through his nose and squirt it out of his eyes through his tear ducts. Don't try this at home . . .

BOO HOO!

Talking of not trying things at home, there's an extraordinary American man named Brad Byers. Not only is he a sword-swallower but he's also known as the Human Toolbox because of his 'ability' to nail a board to his face and drill into his nose with an electric drill. But that's not all! He also offers:

WALKING AND JUMPING ON BROKEN GLASS
– including audience volunteer piggyback ride

FUN WITH A STAPLEGUN – stapling playing
cards to his bare chest, stomach and forehead

BED OF NAILS – lying on a bed of nails with up
to 18 people sitting on top of him

BLOW TORCH – putting out a propane torch
burning at 3,450 degrees on his tongue

TRAPS – putting his hand in a steel trap – with
teeth! – and his tongue in a mousetrap (not
necessarily at the same time . . .)

FAN STOP – stopping a vintage electric fan with
metal blades turning at high speed . . . with his
tongue

TARANTULA/SCORPION BUBBLE-BLOWING
– holding a live spider or scorpion in his mouth
while blowing soap bubbles!

It seems that he's not the only person prepared
to do extraordinary feats in the pursuit of fame.
John Kamakaze, Scotland's self-styled Prince of
Pain, set a strange record a few years ago when

he spent 15 minutes suspended in mid-air from meat hooks embedded in his back. He said it didn't hurt at all.

American highway patrolmen carry gallons of Coke in their vehicles to remove blood from the road after an accident.

There have been instances of extremely obese people having their rectums sucked inside out after flushing aircraft toilets while still sitting on them.

It is possible to cough your guts up.

A woman who had recently visited the South American rainforests began to experience severe pains in her left ear, accompanied by headaches, dizziness and constant rustling sounds. It became so serious that exploratory surgery was required, which revealed that a spider had become trapped in her ear. It had eaten through her eardrum and was living within the aural cavity. The rustling sounds were caused by the spider crawling around inside her skull. The spider's egg sac was also removed.

An entomologist (a scientist who studies insects) was awoken one morning by a tickling sensation, only to find that a 'cockroach's extended mouth parts were imbibing moist nutriment from my nostrils'.

Gary Turner has a very strange party trick. He can pull more than 15 centimetres of skin loose from his neck and forehead and pull them together to cover his whole face. In 2004 he clipped 159 clothes pegs to his face to earn himself a world record.

Every year, over a 1,000 people are bitten by other people in New York city.

When a Tokyo organized-crime boss was killed in 1978, his killers cooked his hands in a pot of soup. They then served this soup to unwitting people. Well, that's one way of destroying the evidence.

A patient in a Danish hospital died as a result of his stomach exploding during an operation. A heated scalpel burned his intestine and ignited stomach gases, which then exploded.

A young police officer from Aberystwyth got so hot when he was on duty that his body temperature reached 41 degrees Celsius (four degrees higher than it should be). His blood literally started to boil.

In 2003 Aron Ralston was trapped by rocks in a canyon. In order to escape and save his life, he had to amputate his lower right arm. He managed to do this by breaking his arm and cutting round the flesh with a blunt knife and pliers, and so survived.

Turn over to see
sneak peeks from other

THAT'S SO
GROSS!
BOOKS

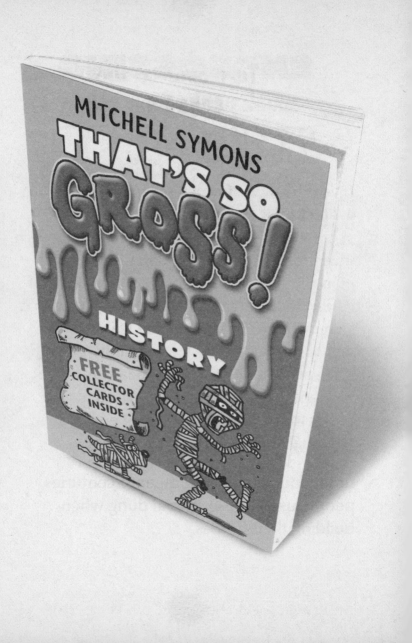

MITCHELL SYMONS

THAT'S SO GROSS!

HISTORY

FREE COLLECTOR CARDS INSIDE

ENGROSSING FUN

Inventors apply for patents in order to protect their inventions. Of course, not every invention leads to a product. One such invention was Adolf A. Neubauer's 1900 plan for a device that fixed to the saddle of a bicycle to deter thieves. It was a spike that shot out from the saddle and stabbed the would-be thief in the bum. Funnily enough, it never took off! A similar idea was used by Frank P. Snow when he devised his hat protector in 1914. It had a spike in the rim. Yup, that should work.

In the fourteenth and fifteenth centuries, people used to use animal dung when building their homes.

According to the writer John Aubrey in his book *Brief Lives*, Edward de Vere, seventeenth Earl of Oxford, was bowing particularly low to Queen Elizabeth I one day when he accidentally broke wind. So embarrassed was he that he went into voluntary exile for seven years. Eventually he returned to court and once again found himself in the presence of the queen. He

bowed carefully this time. The intense silence was only broken by Elizabeth commenting, 'My Lord, I had forgot the fart.'

King Henri IV was one of the most popular French kings, both during and after his reign (from 1589–1610). He showed great care for the welfare of his subjects and displayed an unusual religious tolerance for those days. However, that's not why he appears in this book. No, he's here because he was described as 'smelling like carrion'. When his fiancée met him for the first time, she fainted because of his smell!

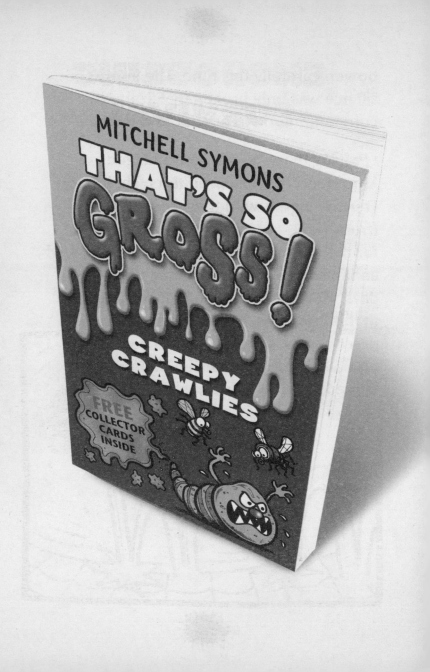

ENGROSSING SURVIVAL

Praying mantises are camouflaged as protection against predators. Their body colour blends with their environment.

When surprised, a barn spider will bounce up and down in the middle of its web – probably in an attempt to look bigger and therefore more threatening.

The markings on the Atlas moth's front wing tips resemble a snake's head – making it look like a frightening target to potential predators.

Stinkbugs ooze a foul smell to protect themselves from their predators. I guess the clue's in the name.

Similarly ladybirds produce a chemical that smells and tastes so terrible that birds and other predators aren't tempted to eat them.

Fire ants have adapted to cope with flooding. When water levels in their nests rise, they form a huge ball with the workers on the outside and the queen inside. This ball then floats, and when it reaches dry land, the ants swarm out and wait for the water to go down.

When the bombardier beetle is threatened by a potential enemy, it sends out a cloud of offensive gas as a defence. This gas is created when two chemicals in its body react in the rear of its abdomen, producing an explosion, which shoots hot gas at the attacker. The beetle can aim its 'cannon' with surprising accuracy.

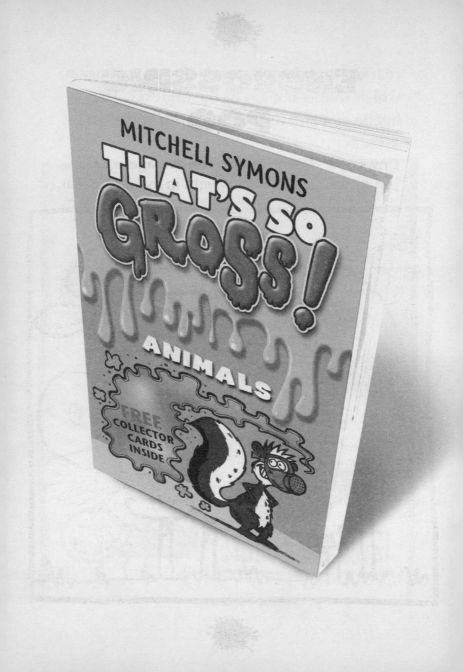

ENGROSSING POO

Cows poo 16 times a day. The average cow produces four times its weight in manure a year.

A male catfish keeps the eggs of his young in his mouth. After they have hatched, if they are in any danger, the father once again opens his huge mouth and lets the youngsters hide inside.

The phrase 'raining cats and dogs' originated in 17th-century England. During heavy downpours

of rain, many cats and dogs unfortunately drowned, and their bodies would be seen floating in the rain torrents that raced through the streets (which didn't, of course, have any drains). This gave rise to the suspicion that it had literally rained 'cats and dogs'.

Mitchell Symons

WHY DOES EAR WAX TASTE SO GROSS?*

. . . and more top trivia!

*stinky ear wax has been hanging around in the ear canal for nearly a month before it is 'pickable'!

Did you know . . .

- **Humans share a third of their DNA with lettuce**

- **Cockroaches fart every fifteen minutes**

- **Giraffes never kneel**

- **The average person spends six months of their life on the loo**

Amaze your mates and fascinate your family with this book packed with jaw-dropping, eyebrow-raising facts!

Mitchell Symons

WHY YOU NEED A PASSPORT WHEN YOU'RE GOING TO PUKE*

. . . and more crazy-but-true facts!

*Puke is the name of a town in Albania. Would YOU like to holiday there . . . ?

Did you know . . .

- **Square watermelons are sold in Japan**

- **There is a River Piddle in Dorset**

- **American use enough toilet paper daily to wrap around the world nine times**

Mitchell Symons goes global – join him on his fun fact-finding world tour!

MITCHELL SYMONS

Do Igloos Have Loos?

Ever wondered . . .

- Why are slugs so slimy?
- Why does your skin go wrinkly in the bath?
- How clever is your right foot?
- What is the best thing to do if you fall into quicksand?
- And do igloos have loos?

Mitchell Symons **knows the** answers . . . and now you will too!

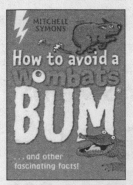

Mitchell Symons
HOW TO AVOID A WOMBAT'S BUM*

And other fascinating facts!

* Don't chase it! Wombats can run up to 25 miles per hour and stop dead in half a stride. They kill their predators this way – the predator runs into the wombat's bumbone and smashes its face.

Amaze and intrigue your friends and family with more fantastic facts and figures:

- Most dinosaurs were no bigger than chickens
- Everton was the first British football club to introduce a stripe down the side of players' shorts
- A snail has about 25,000 teeth
- No piece of paper can be folded in half more than seven times

Just opening this book will have you hooked for hours!

Q: Who writes the best books on farts, bogeys and other yucky stuff?

A: Mitchell Symons, of course

Q: What's his website called?

A: Grossbooks.co.uk, what else!

On this site you can:
- Win cool stuff in quizzes and competitions
- Add your own fab facts and publish them online
- Be first to find out about Mitchell's new books before they're published

As Mitchell's mum would say:
'Thank goodness it's not *scratch 'n' sniff...*'

See for yourself at **Grossbooks.co.uk**